TOIL & DELIVERY

Poems by Bill F. NDI

Langaa Research & Publishing CIG
Mankon, Bamenda

Publisher:

Langaa RPCIG
Langaa Research & Publishing Common Initiative Group
P.O. Box 902 Mankon
Bamenda
North West Region
Cameroon
Langaagrp@gmail.com
www.langaa-rpcig.net

Distributed outside N. America by African Books Collective
orders@africanbookscollective.com
www.africanbookcollective.com

Distributed in N. America by Michigan State University Press
msupress@msu.edu
www.msupress.msu.edu

ISBN: 978-9956-578-18-4

Table of Content

AUTHOR'S NOTES

Why *Toil & Delivery?* Let yourself be charmed, be ensnared, go under the spell of the muse and imagination before enduring the pains of shelling the nuts in which the pleasurable and edible charms are hidden. Be these poems local or global, political or personal, African or non-African, Western/non-Western, about place, politics, women, home, family and religion, be ensnared to birthing and attaching some sense into them. The poems are! They mean what you bring and inject into them. In every poem in this collection each and every reader would find something that talks of/to their condition tickling reflections that tempt and leave non indifferent.

I would like to express sincere gratitude to fellow Australian poet and academic Maria Takolander of Deakin University for her patience in reading and reviewing the poems in this collection in their manuscript form.

FOREWORD

The poems in Bill NDI's *Toil & Delivery* can be as playful and loaded as the clues in a cryptic crossword puzzle, which is to say that they are marked by a strange, energetic hybridity. They occupy a dynamic space between nursery rhyme and visionary Romantic verse, between the colloquial and the archaic, between postmodernity and anachronism. They are local and global, political and personal, Western and non-Western. In 'Paying the price thrice to rice', for example, we read about 'Mother Rice / Thought her a sweet & nice / Mom' who is, in fact, more like 'Nebuchadnezzar in old Babylon'. The poems are about place, politics, women, home, family and religion, and are all grounded in references to the earth, its landscapes, its cycles and its harvests—the sun, the moon, stars, fire, anthills, rice, fruit. Bill F. NDI, whose experience traverses both Africa and the West, is one of those poets who gives meaning to the word globalisation. Bill F. NDI is also a poet who embraces poetry as a material act in a troubled world, even if poetry's power is conveyed with typical irony. 'Strong, strong weak', for example, begins with 'Too strong at picking up a gun / And weak, weak, weak at lifting a pen' and ends with 'Too strong, strong at picking up a pen / And uphill Bully only see in him / Nothing but Job / Grabber / Job / Reincarnated!'

An extraordinary collection with utmost inventiveness which deserves critical attention!

Dr Maria Takolander
Literary Studies and Professional and Creative
Writing
Deakin University

Tyro

In bed

sick

thick

Like a caged baby bird

Thoughts dashed through

Projecting a bitch

That once was!

Her name: Cannon

For she could charge like one

And one day found sick

She had to be put to sleep

And witnessing the putting

Of this sick bitch to sleep

Didn't, on the spot, just bring to sight

This big load to carry

All alone not in a boat

Down into the abbot
U
N
D
E
R
!
Where awaits the boatman!

SANDER & CHRISTER

Sander the explosive

                                                  Christer the positive

Two   good   friends

All in class would theirs stood on ends

And I looked up

And blows I saw fly up

And on each other they fell

And that with me sat not well

As I bring them to question

Was told far from their intention

It was their class'

To see them break the glass

Through which they their friendship

Saw

But with eyes and no saw

Nor sword

Till their classmates' word…!

"Don't ruin that you cherish

Just because others this wish!"

Came from within the voice

And they made their choice

Saying "Sorry!"

"Sorry!"

And with a handshake

The plague

Quaked seeing

Before dying

It's grave

Dug by the grave

Standing their ground

With me at the background!

PAYING THE PRICE THRICE TO RICE

Growing up we delighted in Cultivating rice!

Grown up delighted in seeing the Sun rise!

And heard of Mother Rice

Thought her a sweet & nice

Mom

In whose lexicon

Murder

Hadn't its place for a mother

But like Nebuchadnezzar in old Babylon

 She rules Babylon!

                    With fellow human beings

            In a fix

        And with a P

         Affixing her name

        And greeting her fame!

      With the world paying her thrice

         The price!

dArkness
      road
      and
tomb
one
      reality
one way
pass-
      port
      to
      cross   frontier
          fly
            down
            he-
            !re
                 with light
            obscurantism
                      o
                      l
                  evasion.

My light knows not east nor west
For His rise nor for His nest.

TIME
(6758576)

Bird above the world flying

So high, within you caging

Mystery that rears death

Spurs admiration and would, up

'Bove all thee join where

you like dot display wisdom

And bury mourning at dawn.

SPECTACLES

Nature has insight
One to restore sight,
And envision afore time,
Restore the scum's prime
With or without broom
To allow his freedom to bloom.

THE BROKEN BOND

Chains link us to life

And to it we cling

Ignoring

True warriors, warriors of Peace must

The chains of our physical world break…!

Not until then we are slaves

Lugged around by waves

Like dead leaves

In a stormy sea….!

WHAT DOES IT MATTER?

What does it matter

Taking me for the shadow of matter

Or myself

When in life no elf

Came to show the world that which I am:

A heart that would never pick up an arm?

How does it change the order,

The order of things past, present or

Even the advent of the universe

To pen a verse?

What & where is life?

Is it this stupid jive?

Is it shitty,

Iffy

?

Hic et nunc,

Life is sapid!

And we must sip it!

And we must zip it!

And that's life

For which all should strife!

Like all the others

We are having a lay over

With no thoughts

Of a hang over

Come tomorrow

But of a stronger marrow

And the clock ticks

Like drips from licks

And all we aspire

And discard the mire

Is none but a better

Greasy morrow with butter

To butter whose bread,

When the dire need for children is seen as a threat?

Rise from rags to rugs

From grass to grace

And be schooled in every art of grace

Like Richard Cory

If thou never did wear rags

Then thy end like Cory

Is none but a sorry

Plight

Neither flight

Nor might

Can fight…!

STRONG, STRONG WEAK

Too strong at picking up a gun

And weak, weak, weak at lifting a pen

He like a pendulum swings his forte

And points him at poor little weak Billy

Poor little weak Billy from the foothill

That hosts the colourful anthill

Which in his youth led and won

Him wars against uphill Bully the gun

Carrier.

Too strong, strong at picking up a pen

And uphill Bully only see in him

Nothing but Job

      Grabber

        Job

          Reincarnated!

CHILDHOOD RAIN SHOWERS

Oh! Harmless rain showers

Showers of comfort, love and gentleness

Full of promises

Your caresses

Your music

I crave

And I see

A cloud of tourists

The like of an army

Invading

The Notre Dame Bridge

Under

Each time your drums start

And drive me to thinking

The devil 'mself

Gave them a chase!

And inwardly, I tilt my eyes

To seeing their tinted glass of ignorance!

FRUITS OF BLISS

My star is golden gold

Forever she shines!

Shining!

Attempt not to cloud

Her. Constant

In the like clouds

Aren't; stable, unchanged

And shining always golden gold!

A CHILDLESS FATHER HOPES

Airborne I fly without wings

But continental's

And Every inch away from my boys

I would I fell apart with the voice

And thought of missing a darling

Leaving my mind a ringing

Dazed by sages grown speechless

And I blame not them for I know

Like them my heart is not heartless

Reflections through the gorgeousness

Of the loving kids I sadly miss…!

And here above and humble

In vain, I search for our professed and proclaimed

Greatness and pray these kids

Grow to show mankind this…!

A TRIBUTE TO EVERY MOTHER

The clock ticks

The heart beats

All telling of the passing time

Recalling the sweet incubator

That for months generated heat

For these passing beings

Here, you as well as we are

Here owe her

Divine and heavenly

                              Duties

All hers by right:

Love

          And

                    Cherish

                              Her

                                   Her

                                        Pride…!

See us grow into parenthood

And herself into grand motherhood!

THE UNDERGROUND PARIS

The monsters rarely show up

Trailing the entrails of mother earth

Searing her

        And

           Opening up their mouths

At one end to gulp in

           And at the other

Vomit   out!

To brave the courage

I made this experiment of dying

Before the real…

        A real experience!

That inexpressible gloom on all faces

In her entrails

Driving me home

        Just that sense of life

In the   Grave!

One for the grave-

             Less…!

BORN FREE FREEBORN

Up in the sky

Like a bird flying high

Quest none but a resting

Tree branch

On which to perch

     And

          Hoping

          Having

Found one, must on it land!

BOXING RING

Surprised as a kid,

Was challenge to a boxing duel,

Knowing no ring,

Ringing no bells

Nor having any fuel,

I grabbed a sheet and a pen

And in response said:

"Go thee therefore unto that wall in front

And give 'm as many gibes as thou canst

Until this pen drops…."

The winner shall be History's choice….

In my sleepless rest

On a Paris Street bench

I saw a shadow swagger by

And his gaits in all pride chanted:

                             "I am….

                             I am…."

And my humble inner man

In that sleepless dream

                      Quested: "what?

Or what else other than

One of these shadows walks

And passes by,

Peopling the earth

Not to think of death

With desperate hope they are here to stay…!

TOURIST EXTRAORDINAIRE!

Like a shooting star

From point A to B shooting,

He dashes from village to village

From town to town

From city to city

From country to country

And from continent to continent!

Amazed, a star follows shining

The way shining through the dark

That dark obscurantism

Rooted in their assertion!

COMMEMORATION

Looking at clouds

Cluster in moulds

And sail in sky

Grooms brain spy

To image

Man's voyage

Along whose courses

He fight for causes

To destinations

Unknown with no solutions

To his utter bewilderment

Crystallising the quest for the fate of great men

Who sojourned

And journeyed along

Unnoticed to macrocosm

But to microcosm;

Should one think and know

One unknow_

Able, mystery will become

Placeless in every lexicon…

You may ask why

Such silly thought…? Why?

Simple my response:

Ages before I was,

By the first war

Who shook the world

My sun rose,

By the third's eve, off he dosed.

None saw the sunshine,

I felt it's warmth in mind.

And same date

As today, with no date,

News came my key was lost.

It was not dusk

With abandon, I

Pondered why…!

The absence,

A tree's that in essence,

Constitutes in itself

A forest and falls off.

Walking pass through,

I realised 'twas true

All left was artificial

And nothing natural;

None ever laughed again

But showed their teeth, the laughter, maimed.

Should your sun preciously set,

May I ask… my thought

That stupid

Or the journey worth starting?

It marked not the end of things

Though overturned many things:

Solitude ignited same Friday

And today, Tuesday

Would preciously mark own end

Before my journey's end

For people to look at Biography

Cautioning peace

In Peace

Nursing the import of History.

OUR AWE OBJECTS

In the animal kingdom

Is tortoise's wisdom

While all women,

Irrespective of their patriotic,

Nationalistic, lovable 'n even

Loving feelings, awe even their folk.

PRURIENCE

Home on tree branch

A pear smiles at earth;

Quitting home branch,

In trance, fell a heart

Weighting him leafy,

Which, without comments, sturdy,

In her swatted

And left in mosquito larvae;

The oomph, oops!

Yeast

To raising seeds

From milch pear,

Fruits shall bear.

VOMIT

Experience regurgitates

Unmanliness manifest

In Bray skull

Believing incidental

Grandeur dreamed

Replicates one lived

Though in jungle still

V.I. and fizzling skill

Out of sight,

Smoothened with spicy speech

Mortal sin number one;

Lying....

THE MESSENGER

Little bee
When you buzz
Would you
In the ears
Of the dead;

Wake them from sleep
To come tell us
Of our Mothers:

Were they these
Buzzards in skirts?

And would for them
Little bee drive them

With your magic
            Music
Take them away from the weak;

These weak preys
With graceless praise
Warranting buzzards' life

As they drop out of life

Buzz your music
Till they top the peak!
Little,
Little Bee !

BOB DOWN THAT JOY
(BEYOND THE ORDINARY)

with the loveliest broad face smile

on   the   staircase

three   little   girls

watch on, the case…

one whirls and whirrs

and the   other whimpers

its starkness, dreamed, hosts

gusty squall,

drives home screams and all,

straggly hair strands on ends stand;

with fixity mould's ire on sand budge….

Reality…!

Hallucinations, miles away….!

Smouldering, squeals, screams and screeches

They divide; mould chop them with gusto, smudges…!

His joy bobbed up!

BITCH SONG

In chain to herself,

Rejuvenates

Her song's dawn;

Streaming tears

On her face

Walk appeal.

Ecstatic goes she

Drawing him on the retina

Like slave masters

       Slave masters

Draggled slaves' serfs.

At her

Master

In chain

Holding

Tight at

That end

She laughs

Wags and sings:

"I am, I am

Peptic

Countess'

Duchess'

Empress'

Mistress…"

I WONDER

Why not ten poems

A day in Paris?

Was the interrogation!

I would I could fifty

In an hour

                   Were I not to spend

That running to catch

          The bus

The subway

                    For my job

The course

        And grab a sandwich

                 For a bite…!!

        So goes life in Paris

And so are the fifty

                Per hour poems gone!

        Poems I would

Twelve hundred have done

        A day

Lie buried in this CT

Not the woods in her backyard of yesteryears

Up the Hills of Montmorency

Where centuries ago

Rousseau

Birthed the *Contract*

That engineered the Revolution

That kill the *Contract*

At full revolution

Leaving the streets of Paris

With poems littered

The range of which stretch so far to the grange:

From the gloomy frown in the subway

To the half gloomy grin on the passage way

Such dazzles as would revive Chaucer's May

Stun as to   why   all Parisians   aren't poets…!

THE VOICE OF A RESTING SOUL

When I accepted death my son

You were too poor son

Too poor to offer a drink

Those who clustered around the thing

I'd become; one for the deeps

Or one ready to sail in the sea like ships!

You placed in my hands

To take down to my New Hammock

Two sheets with your mind

In them reading that hyper lucidity

Which stopped people from straining

For my parting after my part playing

And leaving for the young theirs

And I did then acknowledge

Taking cognizance and full knowledge

Of thy plainness of heart

Of the love you did all thy

Span in mine conceal

To give you nothing but this seal

And through it you shall yourself

Humble till the day the self

Gets much of that world and say:

"For that I did enjoy and (h)ate, I must pay."

I loved telling you stories

You loved them and read histories

Of this land to which I now belong

From the time church bells tolled: "ding dong"

Inviting me to saying, in spite of your wishes, "quit"

And you did respond with a saucy word: "shit"

Before admitting good believers (Christians)

Must their mouth shot, maintain

That silence needed by a sleeping man

Especially one like me, in his eternal sleep found!

Taking along my tongue of a teller

I leave you a pen and the soul for a thinker

To set the brains and thoughts

Of gods in Ivory Towers

Flying above like clouds.

Mark! Humble

Your humble self; fish no trouble

Till you your invitation accept

For people to chant you your excerpts

As lullaby

For you are gone by

You shall love

And love

And love your mission

Without concealing your passion

For penning panegyrics

Which like aesthetics

Multiply beauty

Which with its lovely

Caresses smoothens the gentle passing

Like that song we chanted marching

Down the street!

THE WAY TO GO

Parents envisioned education

And told us

They saw him home coming with the best dividend

And dreamily still we did

Ope our ears wide

Like antelopes theirs when danger sensed,

Hoping schooling issues bread winning ticket!

So we started up with education

So did we realise writing

Could be the ticket itself

And to writing we took

Noting crossing the elixir

To salvation

Salvaging poets from their altruisms!

We must cultivate her!

That's why we are poets

CAPTAIN SALUTES ALL

Besides forces artificial,

Are these under Commodore

Who do Donne shall die;

Always on their marks gunning

Down

Honourable owners

of others.

Daniel the wisest

Was not enough to avert commodore's

Wisdom resides in giving him a thought

Sticking to the middle path

And he'll inform thee before visitation

To have thee with courage sail…..

For that lost land we seek is the courageous'

And cowards linger around

To unveil they lack might.

THE UNSEEN

Nobody I assure

Ever me see

Thus I am sure

Not he nor she'll e'er see me

Told is my story when I pass and flow

Turbulently, in my respect, trees bow

Then can I be felt, not seen!

The cool benediction on them pouring.

IN SEARCH FOR IT

Just a blank sheet of paper

It was never taught, my clock.

Green was its music

For its sake, my clock

The pendulum music

Played better.

Its own sound unforgotten,

Dancing but the pendulum tune.

Turning, search I it in the sheets.

Yet, coming it is never.

Return to myself will tarnish all

But Helens say, "return to yourself, farm it ever."

In the cave's under walls

Of what use is it?

Wisdom runs towards our roost.

Chased, hunted and hunting we it find most…!

COMING OF ASH

While hills set on fire in November ablaze,

Trees dance, leaves roll up,

Air current wheezes and chants

And a burning streamside tree in it is thus pushed.

Out's the fire! Light, weak and shriveled, the stem

                                          Floats

The ashes none sees their rise nor fall,

To the bottom have swum 'em

Weeks pass, months die to the near same season,

Like maize visiting the grange in August,

Swims in a cluster,

Breaks open the door, scatters the weeds,

Bathes in the stream

And stops in her its thirst for once for all

As it chants its funeral song!

INFIDELITY IS NOT WOMAN

So sweet and tender

Goaded I was to air out

The only one I could stare at.

She could put out the fire

And were ready to drink me up

When she was or not thirsty

For the practice of the separation

I could not see her on the spot!

Yet, she promised immobility

Which confirms frailty

William's

Appellation of woman!

Well! She is not to blame

For man neither did follow the lane.

THE RETURN HOME

After burden shouldering for years,

Everyone, for rest, goes in homeland.

Approach I my homeland, clad in white

The white of the clouds Rose by the well nourished stream,

Warm, sweet and cold everlasting breeze.

Dumb, deaf and blind I am to any sense.

They scoop one, with me happy in a sedan,

A palanquin, indeed a resting home place.

Why must I in foreign land time waste,

If ants can their nests in the darkest night visit?

Father me sent and now me call'st.

To his company keep, How can I object?

So, to homeland must I go!

Yet, compatriots cease not plaint;

But in homeland furrow must I father seek.

FOR BETTER & ....

Flame consumes mountain.

No extinguisher stopping him,

He gobbles all.

Now, craving fallow by wave-less shores,

Mountain yearns him most, his warmth.

Conscious of efforts to resuscitate death,

Sentient fire is obligated

To turn towards mountain;

Inter one case of infarct

For she harbours ashes,

Fire's offspring, undeniable!

BROOMSTICK

A world on it own!

An instrument to clean;

Yet, for filth,

Cannon to drive

Him into his grave with just one touch.

Insects settle on him

Ignore his might

In tyrants' hands,

The auto-willed supreme of creation,

For broomstick is harmlessly

Deadly !

THE MADMAN SAID:

"A woman who lies

To the husband

With the husband

By the husband

Never procreates

His progenies

Even when he in her lies!"

BIOGRAPHY

This child that was

The man that is

The scriber that will be

The tomorrow's laureate

Looked into the childhood world

The world of adulthood

With surprise and hope

All brought to pass in futility

Through K'cracy;

The turbulence of trees

In the storm

Summarizing life

In which all we need is

Pray in peace

For peace

And if neither can,

Do one for another !

COUNCILORS : *NONFORM*

Skulking belief in child

Stands up mild, not wild

Not until countered

For squatting under the counter

Dreaded not dreading

As he cropped child to awaiting

Blasting Bayonet

Carriers rallying to him magnet;

Chide thy wild weird world

Wild mild child

In heat hid,

Bubble till thou art hit

To breathe fireworks'

Colours of art works

That like one-sided dice

Curbed days and humbled old Great Ozymandias!

In thee, breed like meek viper

That bile to bleed and down any scoffer.

MAILMAN

The thirst for

Life's west end;

The sable goon,

Sleep's elder brother

All long for ladder

To attaining God's home gate

Is shaggy reality for the incinerator

Born of Pol Magpie,

The magnate.

The goon's elder sister

So sweet, silken

Tender and pleasant,

Lulls vexations

When in her, one himself finds

Like a Parisians' eyes

On a quaint yokel.

This the private postman octogenates;

Deserting enveloped anguish,

A box, simian's

In the bank   Across.

MY KEY

Came the key from far away
  The key that could unlock!
  Swam into it left and right;
  Moistened, it opened, I saw the sun's bright.
  Marching from and for where?

This panegyric I must sing
  The key's mark? Stephen!
  Lengthy and greasy he is.
  In his paternal click,
  Pluto he is one knows.

With broad board face mused
  "Be cantonlike and candid,
  My face you'll have. Speed fractures!
  Little drops inundate! Stand by it,
  Your finger you'll never bite!"

Hasty, my head up, ears blocked,
  Not much more any good did it do;

Biting the finger from a slumber,
Took I his words.
Myself, I realized, duped!

Same to my brothers, he bid.
Down you would be dragged, were you hasty in life
They tested it and it happened
Just that I did: retired.
Some bulky fishes they caught.

Stephen the God loving one
Never did he love lies!
Hammer the nail, by it die
He loved not to lie in praise
With untenable weight.

His pupils and children, he read
The way Hughes, Dunbar and Griffin did versify.
Always showing the way forward.
Never done as would our Heads,
In solving a communist's plight.
Stephen, what a father!
God-fearing, child loving, and upright,
Were all plus our heads Stephen?
Oh, what a great height for joy?

O, reverse the order, one cannot.

Staying out of his sight,
  Almost cost me my life.
  But, how could I help it?
  For my future, this, he wanted
  And I could not but wish!

His larynx's vibration to go hunt,
  Hunting those papers
  Which "thine wives they'd be." If not,
  "Progenies if Priapus smiles not.
  Wisdom thine pride not wealth!"

To fertilize his yearnings,
  Set I wandering
  Like tree leaves in Fall
  Falling off a lovable tree
  Only to climb back manure-like.

Yet, just out of decomposition phase one
  And stepping into the second,
  Wishing his leaves broader smiles,
  He set my lachrymal glands at work
  Questioning why he is gone so early.

Knowing he was terrestrial,

One could not but expect such.

Others, weep not with me as good Christians

Respecting this village's tradition

Praying his soul sojourn well!

ACUMEN

Man's Greatness:
The Nothingness
Of All Odds
He Accepts.

MITIGATION (*Plea by a marooned Pen*).

Blessed Poet

Spare that soul

Whose ignorance

In the gutter

Me sent idling,

That rich poor soul !

> Ye rescued me
>
> And with me
>
> Bury him not
>
> Nor in pen, put
>
> Him not like
>
> Would gaolers……

> With thee, in sooth
>
> Would, I pen poems
>
> Slaying not
>
> That poor rich!

Creator poet,

I acknowledge

Thee creator;

For that wisdom,

Work up minds
Pensively fine!

HEROIC ENTERPRISE

Starts like child's play

And seed sown same day,

Ticked the clock over,

Each tick left a hang-over

For two seventy days, all he gathered

And the enterprise confirmed

Him hero some day

After the enterprise father ventured.

He smiled at the world

And stopped to listen

To a new comer mourning

Next cot,

With the twist of a cod

He smiled again

Showing the nothingness of worldly gain.

THE DIRGE

The child I was, heard one chanted.

Its thrill to my father I repeated.

Hailed him its nicety,

Frowned he at my naivety

And his face wrinkled for my poor timing

And my mouth hurried to question:

Why? "You shall know!" did

My mouth seal

And today I would I sing

One

On seeing autocracy buried;

His spectre like my late father's

Hushed me for my trembling mouth

To sing autocracy is there

And not autocracy is dead,

This, his expectation from song-makers;

Panegyric, his gluing sticker.

BARREN DAYS

Vacuum of literary creativity

Nursery of same creativity

Compromise barrenness & fertility

Making a congruous union:

One for the creator

Hardly visible to the eye

'Cos it roams round hearts.

SEA FARING

Everyman adventure

And everywhere

In the forest

On the mountain

On the coast

In the ship

Sails until sails are down

To exit shrunk

And gayest of all beings

For 'tis not forgoable

When sea lion lifts head

As rulers ruling supreme

To reason

And must dive in

For that makes 'm spring stiff.

CALM DOWN

Peace of mind is thy plight

Dwell not in camera to find her

Nor languish over fate's decision

For the content of the womb is unknown

Not until it is unbundled.

Yet, life's success is not in examination

Nor can the reverse be true.

Though 'tis painful and sickening

For pupils to spend years' nights in insomnia

Only hoping for something

In those many years to come,

Which have, to reap yet a thing

We must not stoop low in front of lot

For one never goes off its hands,

Fate's decision must not part us

'Cause we must wage it till the fateful day

We will be needed home

Then shall we part

Each in a sedan to cross

This rugged sea of life.

RIVULET

Stockpile under the crust,

After the rain's tap thrust, it burst.

His pious pavement, he searches.

Continuously, he to the mouth reaches.

But for rebirth, to the mother return,

He never to his source return,

Embracing the ocean as he draws near

With shorter steps than taken first steps, for fear.

DESTINY

On the tarmac, the well pregnant ocean
See I. Miles it stretches far away.
Languidly, draw I near the ocean.
Running, it hurries away....

Higher, higher, higher height!
Undulate me to the ocean meet;
Never my destination make I
Yet, mirages be that I see.

MORPHEUS

In sleep stream
Myself told me
In the wood
Owls hoot.

In bed,
Spell-cast
I eye 'em
With claws
Move close
And withdraw.
Alone
       I groan

Fiction it was
At Morpheus'.

THE CALLER

In darkness, grubs

The eyeless lad to doors

Never to sleep goes he;

Only at doors knock he

To call and choose the best of the time.

With numbed cold hands

He calls like an appetite

Hiding its disfigured silhouette.

Finally, when at any door,

And hungry, he never fails to knock.

With not only one joy are the inhabitants

Left: heads down, dancing left and right,

The eyes rain, the floor drown,

With hands over heads,

He's taken to his last bedroom....!

IRREVOCABLE VOICE

Mature was that fruit, yet unripe for harvest.

That night, at the door he gloated.

Early next morn this voice called.

Neither could he stammer nor wobble.

So, he his roost, made a niche.

At the ceiling, his closed eyes were sailing.

Worked not the lachrymal gland.

For it must have anytime come.

Platitude? He must call men to come.

Gone, never again will he hear the purl.

His loving time keeper halted.

Off is his sun; shunned to shine!

TABLETS OF LIFE

With tenderness, embrace her
And pursue not the unknowable and the unknown
That may spear the heart.
Seek harmony with your surroundings,
Her lovely creatures,
Cast suspicion in the abysm
Like was Lucifer
And his fallen angels.
Then are you sure of life!

Laugh out anguish.
Prostrate to happiness.
When need be create motion
Ascertaining new production
As to grip Life's
Secret in itself, Life!

FOR SURVIVAL

Seeking warmth

In their nest

As they're born

Howl wolf-cubs

Spread on others;

When in her it jumps,

It must stay and strain

To come out wizened

Compensating wolf's whistle....!

WANT

The union is to scoop

The earth; making it palpable.

Bliss is ideal;

One for the ignorant

 And the wealthy.

For the scum, 'tis philosophy

For his smoky marriage

With her, the world,

Is archrival to Samson's

Rewarding a sedulous admiration

For life's highest aspiration

In the   Hereafter.

ASSETS

A man may have a son

To make him shine or shun

For when he grows old 'n blind

The son shall be his eye.

Nature has the sun

Which is not a son

Prickling the mind

To thinking it an eye

For he'll never grow old

Nor shall he radiate cold.

GRANNY FROM A DEEP SLUMBER

Fresh maize and groundnuts eight times dried,

The skies' blue saw'st not ye

And for the journey longed ye the knock and call

Anxiously in that cimmerian eclipse by the squalid door

In ecstasy you are thrown,

Sons, grandchildren and the great-grand ye eye'st

And all on the mountains and valleys under the sun's blades.

The oculist, we extol.

On your soul places not your long longed for friend

Her cold hands, for nil but your beacon I yearned.

Will fall me, if you were snatched, in trance.

Tell me you wait no more for the drab dories.

FIRST AND LAST SPACE

Gulping it? Ever sweet!

At offal expulsion flows sweat

With these moments so happy.

At last it slumps. Stolidity…!

EGG DESTRUCTION

Nine lunar phases after the spray

Cracked and in it fused, comes the prey.

Set is its axis day and night at work.

At full revolution accomplish is the work;

Stop, short it never ticks again!

In a cage, it is planted like a grain!

ON HER NATIVITY

Over is the night, the moon sleeping,

And to sleep goes the owl after this tiresome night

Lighting the birth of the dawn that was and now is.

This morn its eyes ope,

She it did eye

K.M. our hearts burst blooming

With the Spring flower we in November

Missed never.

Yet, nature be divine,

So, to this day, on her,

We our eyes place.

At the brink of th' eclipsed period,

Our heads west setting now does East

And we with her without

Ennui our ecstasy exalt!

Not forgetting that stolidity!

CHASTISEMENT

God inflicts it on man

'Cause he is love,

Loves Satan;

The most obedient of his servants

Sent parking out of heaven

For man's love

To stay in heaven with no rival

This act on men,

Replaces Satan's he buried ages ago!

EQUALITY

Like twins, identical,

This chant's ecclesiastical;

For to lull the under-looked,

Having him hooked,

Just one praise

And the rest disgrace

With smiles

Swimming on files

To inter ignominy of this act;

Parallel Paul's Act.

Mortal

                          Petal

Of earth's Flowers

Yearning followers

To stretch hands

As teacher on pulpit stands

With traditional wisdom

Impervious to exotism in his kingdom

Though, so ardent a preacher

Of equality, this teacher!

THE FEAST

Races on earth

Goad topman

And in the celestial

God on Lucifer feast....

ſTOBIOGRAPHY

ſuteness,

ſy garb

All my life,

Wore out

For me to shout:

'I am'

But my inner man,

My brother

Glimpse in me

In this century

Of the Isms

A drum beater.

Socrates' me

Should be the most dreaded

Yet, my palms' blisters,

My drums' sounds

And the souls pleasure

Maintain SIMA's face....

DELIRIUM

Amidst men

Mean side of men

They think

They feel

They were

The wisest

Of the wise

Perching on others

Not in the order

That is highest

In a dukedom;

The animal's.

AUTOBIOGRAPHY

Muteness,

My garb

All my life,

Wore out

For me to shout:

'I am'

But my inner man,

My brother

Glimpse in me

In this century

Of the Isms

A drum beater.

Socrates' me

Should be the most dreaded

Yet, my palms' blisters,

My drums' sounds

And the souls pleasure

Maintain SIMA's face....